# AIR FRYER MAGIC

*EASY AND TASTY RECIPES FOR ANY MEAL*

# MADIE MERTZ

# Table of Contents

# INTRODUCTION

Welcome to the world of air frying, where delicious meals are made effortlessly and healthily! In this introductory chapter, we'll explore the wonders of air frying and how it has revolutionized the way we cook.

Gone are the days of deep frying in gallons of oil, which not only adds unnecessary calories but also poses health risks. With air frying, you can achieve that same crispy texture and delicious flavor without the guilt. Using hot air circulation, air fryers create a crispy outer layer while locking in moisture, resulting in perfectly cooked dishes every time.

In "Air Fryer Magic: Easy and Tasty Recipes for Any Meal," we'll dive into a treasure trove of recipes spanning breakfast, lunch, dinner, and even snacks and desserts. From crunchy vegetable creations to sizzling steak recipes, and from guilt-free snacking to nutritious nibbles for kids, there's something for everyone in this book.

Whether you're a seasoned air fryer enthusiast or a newcomer to the world of air frying, this book will guide you through the process with simple and easy-to-follow recipes. Get ready to unleash the magic of your air fryer and embark on a culinary journey filled with flavor, convenience, and healthiness. Let's begin cooking up some air fryer magic!

# CHAPTER 1

## GETTING STARTED WITH YOUR AIR FRYER

Welcome to the wonderful world of air frying! In this chapter, we'll delve into the basics of using your air fryer and provide you with essential tips to kickstart your culinary adventures. Whether you're a novice or a seasoned cook, get ready to unlock the magic of your air fryer with simple and delicious recipes that will elevate any meal.

## GETTING ACQUAINTED WITH YOUR AIR FRYER

Before diving into the recipes, it's crucial to familiarize yourself with your air fryer. Here are some fundamental steps to get started:

## Ingredients

- 1. Your favorite food items to air fry (examples: potatoes, chicken wings, vegetables)

- 2. Olive oil or cooking spray

- 3. Salt and pepper (to taste)

Machine Temperature

- Preheat your air fryer to 360°F (180°C) for optimal cooking results.

## Time

- Cooking times may vary depending on the recipe and the size of your air fryer. Refer to specific recipes for precise cooking durations.

## Servings

- Each recipe yields servings for 2-4 people, depending on portion sizes.

# TIPS FOR SUCCESS

1. Preheat Your Air Fryer: Just like with traditional cooking methods, preheating your air fryer ensures even cooking and crispiness.

2. Don't Overcrowd: Give your food ample space in the air fryer basket to allow proper air circulation. Overcrowding can result in unevenly cooked dishes.

3. Use Oil Sparingly: While air frying significantly reduces the need for oil compared to deep frying, a light coating of oil or cooking spray can enhance the crispiness and flavor of your dishes.

4. Shake or Flip: For even cooking, shake the basket or flip the food halfway through the cooking process.

5. Experiment with Seasonings: Get creative with your seasonings to tailor recipes to your taste preferences. Don't be afraid to try new flavor combinations!

Let's Get Cooking!

Now that you're acquainted with your air fryer and armed with essential tips, it's time to embark on your culinary journey. Flip the page to discover a variety of easy and tasty recipes for any meal, from crispy appetizers to mouthwatering mains and delectable desserts. Get ready to experience the magic of air frying like never before!

# CONCLUSION

With these foundational guid

elines, you're well-equipped to make the most out of your air fryer. Whether you're craving classic comfort foods or looking to explore new culinary horizons, your air fryer is your trusty companion for creating delicious meals with ease. So, roll up your sleeves, gather your ingredients, and let the air frying adventures begin!

In the next chapter, we'll dive into appetizers guaranteed to impress your guests and tantalize your taste buds. Get ready to elevate your snacking game with irresistible air-fried delights!

# CHAPTER 2

## ESSENTIAL TOOLS AND INGREDIENTS

In this chapter, we'll explore the essential tools and ingredients you'll need to master the art of air frying. From basic kitchen equipment to key ingredients that will elevate your dishes, let's ensure you're well-prepared to create magic in your air fryer.

## ESSENTIAL TOOLS

Before you start cooking, make sure your kitchen is equipped with these essential tools:

1. Air Fryer: Of course, the star of the show! Choose a reliable air fryer that suits your cooking needs and fits your kitchen space.

2. Measuring Cups and Spoons: Precise measurements are crucial for achieving consistent results in your recipes.

3. Kitchen Tongs: Perfect for flipping food items and removing them from the air fryer basket.

4. Oil Mister or Cooking Spray: Use for lightly coating food with oil to enhance crispiness.

5. Parchment Paper or Aluminum Foil: Optional, but useful for lining the air fryer basket to prevent sticking, especially for delicate items.

6. Kitchen Timer: Ensure your dishes are cooked to perfection by keeping track of cooking times.

7. Instant-Read Thermometer: Useful for checking the internal temperature of meats and ensuring they're cooked safely.

**Essential Ingredients**

Stock up your pantry with these essential ingredients to create a variety of delicious air-fried dishes:

1. Olive Oil: A versatile cooking oil that adds flavor

and crispiness to your dishes.

2. Salt and Pepper: Basic seasonings to enhance the taste of your food.

3. Garlic Powder: Adds a savory flavor to meats, vegetables, and snacks.

4. Paprika: Provides a subtle smokiness and color to your dishes.

5. Breadcrumbs or Panko: Use for coating meats and vegetables for extra crunch.

6. All-Purpose Flour: Essential for dredging and coating food items before air frying.

7. Eggs: Used as a binding agent when breading food items.

8. Fresh Herbs: Elevate the flavor profile of your dishes with herbs like rosemary, thyme, and parsley.

9. Parmesan Cheese: Adds a salty, nutty flavor and crispy texture to dishes.

10. Honey or Maple Syrup: Perfect for adding a touch of sweetness to savory dishes or glazing meats.

## Machine Temperature and Time

Refer to individual recipes for specific machine temperatures and cooking times, as they may vary depending on the dish. However, as a general guideline:

- Preheat your air fryer to temperatures ranging from 350°F to 400°F (175°C to 200°C) for most recipes.

- Cooking times typically range from 8 to 20 minutes, depending on the recipe and the size/thickness of the food items.

- Remember to shake the air fryer basket or flip the food halfway through the cooking time for even browning and crispiness.

Servings

Recipes in this book are designed to serve 2 to 4 people, depending on portion sizes. Adjust ingredients accordingly for larger or smaller servings.

# CONCLUSION

Armed with the essential tools and ingredients outlined in this chapter, you're ready to embark on your air frying journey with confidence. Whether you're craving crispy chicken wings, golden French fries, or succulent roasted vegetables, your air fryer will be your faithful companion in creating easy and tasty meals for any occasion.

In the following chapters, we'll dive into a treasure trove of recipes designed to showcase the versatility and convenience of air frying. Get ready to tantalize your taste buds and impress your family and friends with a wide array of mouthwatering dishes!

Next up, we'll explore appetizers guaranteed to kickstart any meal with flavor and flair. Get ready to elevate your snacking game with these irresistible air-fried delights!

# CHAPTER 3

## BREAKFAST DELIGHTS

Welcome to the most important meal of the day—breakfast! In this chapter, we'll explore a variety of delicious breakfast recipes that you can easily whip up using your air fryer. From classic morning staples to inventive creations, get ready to start your day on a flavorful note with these breakfast delights.

## CLASSIC AIR FRYER FRENCH TOAST STICKS

**Ingredients:**

- 4 slices of bread (white or whole wheat)

- 2 eggs

- 1/4 cup milk

- 1 teaspoon vanilla extract

- 1/2 teaspoon cinnamon

- Maple syrup, for serving

**Machine Temperature:**

- Preheat your air fryer to 360°F (180°C).

**Time:**

- Cook for 6-8 minutes, flipping halfway through, until golden brown.

**Servings:**

- Serves 2.

# CRISPY AIR FRYER BREAKFAST POTATOES

**Ingredients:**

- 2 large potatoes, diced into cubes

- 2 tablespoons olive oil

- 1 teaspoon garlic powder

- 1 teaspoon paprika

- Salt and pepper to taste

- Fresh parsley, chopped (for garnish)

**Machine Temperature:**

- Preheat your air fryer to 380°F (190°C).

**Time:**

- Cook for 15-20 minutes, shaking the basket halfway through, until potatoes are crispy and golden brown.

**Servings:**

- Serves 4.

# AIR FRIED BREAKFAST BURRITOS

**Ingredients:**

- 4 large flour tortillas

- 4 eggs, scrambled

- 1 cup cooked breakfast sausage or bacon, chopped

- 1/2 cup shredded cheddar cheese

- Salt and pepper to taste

- Salsa and sour cream, for serving (optional)

**Machine Temperature:**

- Preheat your air fryer to 360°F (180°C).

**Time:**

- Cook for 5-6 minutes until the tortillas are crispy

and golden brown.

**Servings:**

- Serves 4.

# BLUEBERRY AIR FRYER MUFFINS

**Ingredients:**

- 1 1/2 cups all-purpose flour

- 1/2 cup granulated sugar

- 2 teaspoons baking powder

- 1/2 teaspoon salt

- 1/2 cup milk

- 1/4 cup vegetable oil

- 1 egg

- 1 cup fresh blueberries

**Machine Temperature:**

- Preheat your air fryer to 320°F (160°C).

**Time:**

- Cook for 10-12 minutes until a toothpick inserted into the center comes out clean.

**Servings:**

- Makes 6 muffins.

# CONCLUSION

Start your mornings off right with these delectable air fryer breakfast recipes. Whether you're in the mood for something sweet like French toast sticks or savory like crispy breakfast potatoes, your air fryer has got you covered. With minimal effort and maximum flavor, these breakfast delights are sure to become favorites in your household.

In the next chapter, we'll explore lunchtime favorites that you can easily prepare using your air fryer. Get ready to upgrade your lunch game with mouthwatering recipes that are both convenient and delicious!

# CHAPTER 4

## APPETIZERS AND SNACKS

Get ready to elevate your snacking game with these irresistible appetizers and snacks cooked to perfection in your air fryer. From crispy classics to creative bites, these recipes will tantalize your taste buds and impress your guests. Let's dive into a world of flavor and convenience with these air fryer delights!

## CRUNCHY AIR FRYER MOZZARELLA STICKS

**Ingredients:**

- 12 mozzarella cheese sticks

- 1 cup Italian breadcrumbs

- 2 eggs, beaten

- 1/2 cup all-purpose flour

- Marinara sauce, for dipping

**Machine Temperature:**

- Preheat your air fryer to 380°F (190°C).

**Time:**

- Cook for 6-8 minutes until golden and crispy.

**Servings:**

- Serves 4.

# CRISPY PARMESAN ZUCCHINI FRIES

**Ingredients:**

- 2 medium zucchinis, cut into fries

- 1/2 cup grated Parmesan cheese

- 1/2 cup breadcrumbs

- 1 teaspoon garlic powder

- 1/2 teaspoon dried oregano

- Salt and pepper to taste

- Marinara sauce or ranch dressing, for dipping

**Machine Temperature:**

- Preheat your air fryer to 400°F (200°C).

**Time:**

- Cook for 10-12 minutes until golden and crispy.

**Servings:**

- Serves 4.

# FLAVORFUL AIR FRYER BUFFALO CAULIFLOWER BITES

## Ingredients:

- 1 head cauliflower, cut into florets

- 1/2 cup all-purpose flour

- 1/2 cup milk

- 1 teaspoon garlic powder

- Salt and pepper to taste

- 1/2 cup buffalo sauce

- 2 tablespoons melted butter or olive oil

- Ranch or blue cheese dressing, for dipping

## Machine Temperature:

- Preheat your air fryer to 375°F (190°C).

## Time:

- Cook for 15-20 minutes, shaking the basket halfway through, until cauliflower is crispy and tender.

**Servings:**

- Serves 4.

# SAVORY AIR FRYER STUFFED MUSHROOMS

## Ingredients:

- 12 large mushrooms, stems removed and reserved

- 1/2 cup Italian sausage, cooked and crumbled

- 1/4 cup breadcrumbs

- 1/4 cup grated Parmesan cheese

- 2 tablespoons chopped fresh parsley

- 2 cloves garlic, minced

- Salt and pepper to taste

## Machine Temperature:

- Preheat your air fryer to 360°F (180°C).

## Time:

- Cook for 8-10 minutes until mushrooms are tender and filling is golden brown.

## Servings:

- Serves 4.

# CONCLUSION

With these mouthwatering appetizers and snacks, you'll be the star of any gathering. From cheesy mozzarella sticks to crispy cauliflower bites, your air fryer makes it easy to whip up crowd-pleasing treats in no time. Enjoy these flavorful bites as starters, party snacks, or anytime indulgences!

In the next chapter, we'll explore hearty and satisfying dinner recipes that are sure to please the whole family. Get ready to transform your dinner table with these easy and delicious air fryer meals!

# CHAPTER 5

## CRUNCHY VEGETABLE CREATIONS

In this chapter, we'll celebrate the versatility of vegetables by transforming them into irresistibly crunchy creations in your air fryer. Whether you're looking for tasty sides or satisfying mains, these vegetable-centric recipes will add a burst of flavor and texture to your meals. Get ready to indulge in a delicious array of crispy vegetable delights!

## CRISPY AIR FRYER BRUSSELS SPROUTS, TRIMMED AND HALVED

**Ingredients:**

- 1 lb Brussels s

- 2 tablespoons olive oil

- 2 cloves garlic, minced

- Salt and pepper to taste

- Balsamic glaze, for drizzling (optional)

**Machine Temperature:**

- Preheat your air fryer to 375°F (190°C).

**Time:**

- Cook for 15-20 minutes, shaking the basket halfway through, until Brussels sprouts are crispy and golden brown.

- Serves 4.

# ZESTY AIR FRYER SWEET POTATO FRIES

**Ingredients:**

- 2 large sweet potatoes, cut into fries

- 2 tablespoons olive oil

- 1 teaspoon paprika

- 1/2 teaspoon garlic powder

- 1/2 teaspoon cumin

- Salt and pepper to taste

- Chipotle aioli or sriracha mayo, for dipping

**Machine Temperature:**

- Preheat your air fryer to 400°F (200°C).

**Time:**

- Cook for 18-20 minutes, shaking the basket halfway through, until sweet potato fries are crispy and tender.

**Servings:**

- Serves 4.

# CRUNCHY AIR FRIED GREEN BEANS

**Ingredients:**

- 1 lb green beans, trimmed

- 2 tablespoons grated Parmesan cheese

- 1 tablespoon olive oil

- 1/2 teaspoon garlic powder

- Salt and pepper to taste

- Lemon wedges, for serving

**Machine Temperature:**

- Preheat your air fryer to 380°F (190°C).

**Time:**

- Cook for 10-12 minutes until green beans are crispy and slightly blistered.

**Servings:**

- Serves 4.

# GOLDEN AIR FRYER CAULIFLOWER "WINGS"

**Ingredients:**

- 1 head cauliflower, cut into florets

- 1/2 cup all-purpose flour

- 1/2 cup milk or plant-based milk

- 1 teaspoon garlic powder

- 1/2 teaspoon paprika

- Salt and pepper to taste

- Buffalo sauce or barbecue sauce, for tossing

**Machine Temperature:**

- Preheat your air fryer to 400°F (200°C).

**Time:**

- Cook for 18-20 minutes, shaking the basket halfway through, until cauliflower is crispy and golden.

**Servings:**

- Serves 4.

# CONCLUSION

Who says vegetables have to be boring? With these crunchy vegetable creations, you'll discover a whole new world of flavor and texture. From crispy Brussels sprouts to zesty sweet potato fries, your air fryer makes it easy to enjoy delicious and nutritious vegetable dishes that the whole family will love.

In the next chapter, we'll explore comforting and satisfying dinner recipes that are perfect for any occasion. Get ready to delight your taste buds with hearty meals made effortlessly in your air fryer!

# CHAPTER 6

## CRISPY CHICKEN DISHES

Prepare to indulge in the ultimate comfort food with these mouthwatering crispy chicken dishes cooked to perfection in your air fryer. From classic favorites to inventive twists, these recipes will satisfy your cravings for juicy, tender chicken with a perfectly crispy exterior. Let's dive into a world of flavor and crunch with these irresistible chicken creations!

## CLASSIC AIR FRYER FRIED CHICKEN

**Ingredients:**

- 4 bone-in, skin-on chicken thighs

- 1 cup all-purpose flour

- 1 teaspoon paprika

- 1 teaspoon garlic powder

- 1 teaspoon onion powder

- Salt and pepper to taste

- Cooking spray

**Machine Temperature:**

- Preheat your air fryer to 380°F (190°C).

**Time:**

- Cook for 25-30 minutes, flipping halfway through, until chicken is golden brown and cooked through.

**Servings:**

- Serves 2.

# CRISPY AIR FRIED CHICKEN TENDERS

**Ingredients:**

- 1 lb chicken tenders

- 1 cup panko breadcrumbs

- 1/2 cup grated Parmesan cheese

- 1 teaspoon garlic powder

- 1 teaspoon paprika

- Salt and pepper to taste

- BBQ sauce or honey mustard, for dipping

**Machine Temperature:**

- Preheat your air fryer to 400°F (200°C).

**Time:**

- Cook for 10-12 minutes until chicken tenders are golden and crispy.

**Servings:**

- Serves 4.

# FLAVORFUL AIR FRYER CHICKEN WINGS

**Ingredients:**

- 2 lbs chicken wings, split into flats and drumettes

- 2 tablespoons baking powder

- 1 teaspoon garlic powder

- 1 teaspoon paprika

- Salt and pepper to taste

- Buffalo sauce or barbecue sauce, for tossing

**Machine Temperature:**

- Preheat your air fryer to 380°F (190°C).

**Time:**

- Cook for 25-30 minutes, shaking the basket halfway through, until chicken wings are crispy and cooked through.

**Servings:**

- Serves 4.

# CRUNCHY AIR FRYER CHICKEN PARMESAN

**Ingredients:**

- 4 boneless, skinless chicken breasts

- 1 cup Italian breadcrumbs

- 1/2 cup grated Parmesan cheese

- 1 egg, beaten

- 1 cup marinara sauce

- 1 cup shredded mozzarella cheese

- Fresh basil leaves, for garnish

**Machine Temperature:**

- Preheat your air fryer to 400°F (200°C).

**Time:**

- Cook for 12-15 minutes until chicken is cooked through and cheese is melted and bubbly.

**Servings:**

- Serves 4.

# CONCLUSION

With these crispy chicken dishes, you'll never have to choose between juicy meat and crunchy coating again. From classic fried chicken to flavorful chicken Parmesan, your air fryer makes it easy to enjoy your favorite chicken recipes without the excess oil and mess. Get ready to savor every crispy bite!

In the next chapter, we'll explore delightful dessert recipes that you can easily prepare using your air fryer. Get ready to satisfy your sweet tooth with these irresistible treats!

# CHAPTER 7
## SEAFOOD SENSATIONS

Welcome to a culinary voyage through the seas!

In this chapter, we'll dive into the delectable world of seafood sensations made easy and tasty with your air fryer. From crispy shrimp to succulent fish fillets, get ready to tantalize your taste buds with these flavorful and fuss-free recipes that celebrate the bounty of the ocean.

## CRISPY COCONUT SHRIMP

**Ingredients:**

- 1 lb large shrimp, peeled and deveined

- 1 cup shredded coconut

- 1 cup panko breadcrumbs

- 2 eggs, beaten

- Salt and pepper to taste

- Sweet chili sauce, for dipping

**Machine Temperature:**

- Preheat your air fryer to 380°F (190°C).

**Time:**

- Cook for 8-10 minutes until shrimp are golden and crispy.

**Servings:**

- Serves 4.

# LEMON GARLIC AIR FRYER SALMON

**Ingredients:**

- 4 salmon fillets

- 2 tablespoons olive oil

- 2 cloves garlic, minced

- Zest of 1 lemon

- Juice of 1 lemon

- Salt and pepper to taste

- Fresh parsley, for garnish

- Lemon wedges, for serving

**Machine Temperature:**

- Preheat your air fryer to 400°F (200°C).

**Time:**

- Cook for 10-12 minutes until salmon is cooked through and flakes easily with a fork.

**Servings:**

- Serves 4.

# CRISPY FISH TACOS

**Ingredients:**

- 1 lb white fish fillets (such as cod or tilapia), cut into strips

- 1/2 cup all-purpose flour

- 2 eggs, beaten

- 1 cup panko breadcrumbs

- 1 teaspoon chili powder

- 1/2 teaspoon garlic powder

- Salt and pepper to taste

- Corn tortillas, for serving

- Shredded cabbage, diced tomatoes, avocado slices, and lime wedges, for topping

**Machine Temperature:**

- Preheat your air fryer to 380°F (190°C).

**Time:**

- Cook for 8-10 minutes until fish is golden and crispy.

**Servings:**

- Serves 4.

# HERB-CRUSTED AIR FRYER SCALLOPS

**Ingredients:**

- 1 lb scallops, patted dry

- 1/2 cup breadcrumbs

- 1/4 cup grated Parmesan cheese

- 2 tablespoons chopped fresh parsley

- 1 teaspoon garlic powder

- Salt and pepper to taste

- Lemon wedges, for serving

**Machine Temperature:**

- Preheat your air fryer to 400°F (200°C).

**Time:**

- Cook for 6-8 minutes until scallops are golden and cooked through.

**Servings:**

- Serves 4.

# CONCLUSION

Experience the flavors of the ocean with these seafood sensations made easy and delicious in your air fryer. Whether you're craving crispy coconut shrimp, succulent salmon, or flavorful fish tacos, these recipes are sure to satisfy your seafood cravings. Prepare to embark on a culinary adventure and savor every bite!

In the final chapter, we'll explore tips and tricks for mastering your air fryer and unleashing your culinary creativity. Get ready to elevate your cooking game and enjoy endless possibilities in the kitchen!

# CHAPTER 8

## FLAVORFUL BEEF RECIPES

In this chapter, we'll explore the rich and savory world of beef dishes cooked to perfection in your air fryer. From juicy burgers to tender steak bites, these flavorful recipes will satisfy your cravings for hearty and satisfying meals. Get ready to savor the deliciousness of beef with these easy and tasty recipes!

## JUICY AIR FRYER HAMBURGERS

**Ingredients:**

- 1 lb ground beef

- 1/4 cup breadcrumbs

- 1 egg

- 1 teaspoon Worcestershire sauce

- 1/2 teaspoon garlic powder

- Salt and pepper to taste

- Burger buns and your favorite toppings

**Machine Temperature:**

- Preheat your air fryer to 375°F (190°C).

**Time:**

- Cook for 10-12 minutes, flipping halfway through, until burgers are cooked to your desired level of doneness.

**Servings:**

- Makes 4 burgers.

# TENDER AIR FRIED STEAK BITES

**Ingredients:**

- 1 lb beef sirloin or ribeye steak, cut into bite-sized pieces

- 2 tablespoons olive oil

- 1 teaspoon garlic powder

- 1 teaspoon smoked paprika

- Salt and pepper to taste

- Steak sauce or chimichurri, for dipping

**Machine Temperature:**

- Preheat your air fryer to 400°F (200°C).

## Time:

- Cook for 8-10 minutes until steak bites are browned and cooked to your preferred level of doneness.

## Servings:

- Serves 4.

# CRISPY AIR FRYER BEEF TAQUITOS

## Ingredients:

- 1 lb ground beef

- 1/2 cup diced onion

- 2 cloves garlic, minced

- 1 teaspoon chili powder

- 1/2 teaspoon cumin

- Salt and pepper to taste

- 12 small flour or corn tortillas

- Cooking spray

- Salsa, guacamole, and sour cream, for serving

## Machine Temperature:

- Preheat your air fryer to 380°F (190°C).

**Time:**

- Cook for 8-10 minutes until taquitos are golden and crispy.

**Servings:**

- Makes 12 taquitos.

# FLAVORFUL AIR FRIED BEEF STIR FRY

**Ingredients:**

- 1 lb beef sirloin, thinly sliced

- 2 tablespoons soy sauce

- 1 tablespoon hoisin sauce

- 1 tablespoon sesame oil

- 1 teaspoon minced ginger

- 2 cloves garlic, minced

- 1 cup broccoli florets

- 1 bell pepper, sliced

- 1/2 cup sliced carrots

- Cooked rice, for serving

**Machine Temperature:**

- Preheat your air fryer to 400°F (200°C).

**Time:**

- Cook for 10-12 minutes, stirring halfway through, until beef is cooked through and vegetables are tender-crisp.

**Servings:**

- Serves 4.

# CONCLUSION

With these flavorful beef recipes, you'll enjoy delicious and satisfying meals cooked with ease in your air fryer. Whether you're in the mood for juicy burgers, tender steak bites, crispy taquitos, or a savory stir fry, these recipes are sure to delight your taste buds and impress your family and friends. Get ready to enjoy the magic of beef dishes made effortlessly in your air fryer!

# CHAPTER 9

## PORK PERFECTION

In this chapter, we'll uncover the secrets to achieving pork perfection in your air fryer. From succulent chops to crispy bacon, these recipes will showcase the versatility and flavor of pork in all its glory. Get ready to elevate your meals with these easy and tasty pork dishes!

## JUICY AIR FRYER PORK CHOPS

**Ingredients:**

- 4 pork chops, bone-in or boneless

- 2 tablespoons olive oil

- 1 teaspoon garlic powder

- 1 teaspoon paprika

- Salt and pepper to taste

- Fresh herbs for garnish (optional)

**Machine Temperature:**

- Preheat your air fryer to 400°F (200°C).

## Time:

- Cook for 12-15 minutes, flipping halfway through, until pork chops reach an internal temperature of 145°F (63°C).

## Servings:

- Serves 4.

# CRISPY AIR FRIED PORK BELLY BITES

## Ingredients:

- 1 lb pork belly, cut into bite-sized pieces

- 1 tablespoon soy sauce

- 1 tablespoon hoisin sauce

- 1 teaspoon five-spice powder

- 1/2 teaspoon garlic powder

- Salt and pepper to taste

- Green onions, thinly sliced, for garnish

## Machine Temperature:

- Preheat your air fryer to 400°F (200°C).

**Time:**

- Cook for 20-25 minutes until pork belly is crispy and caramelized.

**Servings:**

- Serves 4.

# FLAVORFUL AIR FRYER PORK TENDERLOIN

**Ingredients:**

- 1 lb pork tenderloin

- 2 tablespoons olive oil

- 2 cloves garlic, minced

- 1 teaspoon dried thyme

- 1 teaspoon dried rosemary

- Salt and pepper to taste

- Dijon mustard for serving

**Machine Temperature:**

- Preheat your air fryer to 375°F (190°C).

**Time:**

- Cook for 18-20 minutes until pork tenderloin reaches an internal temperature of 145°F (63°C).

**Servings:**

- Serves 4.

# CRISPY AIR FRYER PORK SCHNITZEL

**Ingredients:**

- 4 pork cutlets

- 1/2 cup all-purpose flour

- 2 eggs, beaten

- 1 cup breadcrumbs

- 1 teaspoon paprika

- 1/2 teaspoon garlic powder

- Salt and pepper to taste

- Lemon wedges for serving

**Machine Temperature:**

- Preheat your air fryer to 380°F (190°C).

**Time:**

- Cook for 10-12 minutes until pork schnitzel is

golden and crispy.

**Servings:**

- Serves 4.

# CONCLUSION

With these pork perfection recipes, you'll enjoy tender, juicy, and flavorful pork dishes that are easy to make in your air fryer. Whether you're craving succulent pork chops, crispy pork belly bites, tenderloin, or schnitzel, these recipes are sure to please your taste buds and impress your guests. Get ready to savor the magic of pork prepared effortlessly in your air fryer!

In the final chapter, we'll wrap up our culinary journey with tips and tricks for mastering your air fryer and creating your own delicious recipes. Get ready to unleash your creativity in the kitchen!

# CHAPTER 10

## DELECTABLE LAMB AND VEAL

In this final chapter, we'll explore the luxurious flavors of lamb and veal cooked to perfection in your air fryer. From tender chops to savory meatballs, these recipes will elevate your dining experience with their rich and delectable taste. Get ready to indulge in the elegance of lamb and veal with these easy and tasty recipes!

## SUCCULENT AIR FRYER LAMB CHOPS

**Ingredients:**

- 4 lamb chops

- 2 tablespoons olive oil

- 2 cloves garlic, minced

- 1 teaspoon dried rosemary

- 1 teaspoon dried thyme

- Salt and pepper to taste

- Lemon wedges for serving

**Machine Temperature:**

- Preheat your air fryer to 400°F (200°C).

**Time:**

- Cook for 12-15 minutes until lamb chops reach an internal temperature of 145°F (63°C) for medium-rare.

**Servings:**

- Serves 2.

# FLAVORFUL AIR FRIED LAMB MEATBALLS

**Ingredients:**

- 1 lb ground lamb

- 1/4 cup breadcrumbs

- 1 egg

- 2 cloves garlic, minced

- 1 teaspoon dried oregano

- 1 teaspoon ground cumin

- Salt and pepper to taste

- Tzatziki sauce for serving

**Machine Temperature:**

- Preheat your air fryer to 380°F (190°C).

**Time:**

- Cook for 10-12 minutes until meatballs are cooked through and golden brown.

**Servings:**

- Makes about 12 meatballs.

# TENDER AIR FRYER VEAL CUTLETS

**Ingredients:**

- 4 veal cutlets

- 1/2 cup all-purpose flour

- 2 eggs, beaten

- 1 cup breadcrumbs

- 1 teaspoon dried thyme

- 1 teaspoon garlic powder

- Salt and pepper to taste

- Lemon wedges for serving

**Machine Temperature:**

- Preheat your air fryer to 380°F (190°C).

**Time:**

- Cook for 8-10 minutes until veal cutlets are golden and crispy.

**Servings:**

- Serves 4.

# CRISPY VEAL MILANESE

**Ingredients:**

- 4 veal cutlets

- 1/2 cup all-purpose flour

- 2 eggs, beaten

- 1 cup breadcrumbs

- 1/2 cup grated Parmesan cheese

- 1 teaspoon dried oregano

- 1 teaspoon garlic powder

- Salt and pepper to taste

- Lemon wedges and arugula salad for serving

**Machine Temperature:**

- Preheat your air fryer to 380°F (190°C).

**Time:**

- Cook for 10-12 minutes until veal is cooked through and breadcrumbs are golden and crispy.

**Servings:**

- Serves 4.

# CONCLUSION

With these delectable lamb and veal recipes, you'll enjoy a luxurious dining experience right in the comfort of your own home. Whether you're craving succulent lamb chops, flavorful meatballs, or crispy veal cutlets, your air fryer makes it easy to achieve perfect results every time. Indulge in the elegance of these dishes and treat yourself to a memorable meal!

Thank you for joining me on this culinary journey through the magic of air frying. I hope this book has inspired you to explore new flavors, get creative in the kitchen, and enjoy delicious meals with family and friends. Happy cooking!

# CHAPTER 11

## MEATLESS MARVELS

In this chapter, we'll celebrate the versatility and deliciousness of meatless meals prepared in your air fryer. Whether you're a dedicated vegetarian or simply looking to incorporate more plant-based options into your diet, these recipes will delight your taste buds and showcase the incredible flavors of vegetables, tofu, and more. Get ready to be amazed by these meatless marvels!

## CRISPY AIR FRIED TOFU NUGGETS

**Ingredients:**

- 1 block extra-firm tofu, pressed and cubed

- 1/4 cup soy sauce

- 2 tablespoons maple syrup

- 1 teaspoon garlic powder

- 1 teaspoon smoked paprika

- 1 cup breadcrumbs

- Salt and pepper to taste

- Barbecue sauce or dipping sauce of your choice

**Machine Temperature:**

- Preheat your air fryer to 380°F (190°C).

**Time:**

- Cook for 15-20 minutes until tofu nuggets are crispy and golden brown.

**Servings:**

- Serves 4.

# FLAVORFUL AIR FRYER VEGGIE BURGER PATTIES

**Ingredients:**

- 1 can black beans, drained and rinsed

- 1 cup cooked quinoa

- 1/2 cup breadcrumbs

- 1/4 cup chopped onion

- 1/4 cup chopped bell pepper

- 1 teaspoon cumin

- 1 teaspoon chili powder

- Salt and pepper to taste

- Burger buns and toppings of your choice

**Machine Temperature:**

- Preheat your air fryer to 375°F (190°C).

**Time:**

- Cook for 10-12 minutes, flipping halfway through, until veggie burger patties are heated through and crispy on the outside.

**Servings:**

- Makes 4 patties.

# CRISPY AIR FRIED CAULIFLOWER WINGS

**Ingredients:**

- 1 head cauliflower, cut into florets

- 1/2 cup all-purpose flour

- 1/2 cup milk or plant-based milk

- 1 teaspoon garlic powder

- Salt and pepper to taste

- 1 cup breadcrumbs

- Buffalo sauce or barbecue sauce for tossing

**Machine Temperature:**

- Preheat your air fryer to 400°F (200°C).

**Time:**

- Cook for 15-18 minutes until cauliflower wings are crispy and golden.

**Servings:**

- Serves 4.

# CRUNCHY AIR FRYER FALAFEL

**Ingredients:**

- 1 can chickpeas, drained and rinsed

- 1/4 cup chopped onion

- 2 cloves garlic, minced

- 2 tablespoons chopped fresh parsley

- 1 teaspoon ground cumin

- 1 teaspoon ground coriander

- 1/2 teaspoon baking powder

- Salt and pepper to taste

- Tahini sauce for serving

**Machine Temperature:**

- Preheat your air fryer to 380°F (190°C).

**Time:**

- Cook for 12-15 minutes until falafel is crispy and golden brown.

**Servings:**

- Makes about 12 falafel balls.

# CONCLUSION

With these meatless marvels, you'll discover a world of flavor and creativity that doesn't rely on meat. From crispy tofu nuggets to flavorful veggie burger patties, your air fryer opens up endless possibilities for delicious and satisfying vegetarian meals. Whether you're cooking for Meatless Mondays or embracing a plant-based lifestyle, these recipes are sure to satisfy even the most discerning palate.

# CHAPTER 12

## AIR-FRIED SANDWICHES AND WRAPS

In this chapter, we'll revolutionize your lunchtime routine with a collection of delicious sandwiches and wraps that are cooked to perfection in your air fryer. From gooey grilled cheese to crispy wraps, these recipes are guaranteed to elevate your sandwich game and satisfy your cravings. Get ready to enjoy easy and tasty meals with these air-fried delights!

## CRISPY AIR FRYER GRILLED CHEESE SANDWICH

**Ingredients:**

- 4 slices of bread

- 1 cup shredded cheese (such as cheddar or mozzarella)

- 2 tablespoons butter, softened

**Machine Temperature:**

- Preheat your air fryer to 360°F (180°C).

## Time:

- Cook for 4-6 minutes, flipping halfway through, until bread is golden and cheese is melted.

## Servings:

- Makes 2 sandwiches.

# CRUNCHY AIR FRIED CHICKEN CAESAR WRAP

## Ingredients:

- 2 large tortillas (whole wheat or spinach)

- 1 cup cooked chicken breast, sliced or shredded

- 1/2 cup romaine lettuce, chopped

- 2 tablespoons grated Parmesan cheese

- 2 tablespoons Caesar dressing

- Salt and pepper to taste

## Machine Temperature:

- Preheat your air fryer to 380°F (190°C).

## Time:

- Cook for 3-4 minutes until the wrap is crispy and heated through.

**Servings:**

- Makes 2 wraps.

# FLAVORFUL AIR FRYER FALAFEL PITA POCKETS

## Ingredients:

- 2 pita pockets, halved

- 6 homemade or store-bought falafel balls

- 1/2 cup shredded lettuce

- 1/4 cup diced tomatoes

- 1/4 cup diced cucumbers

- Tahini sauce or yogurt sauce for drizzling

## Machine Temperature:

- Preheat your air fryer to 380°F (190°C).

## Time:

- Cook for 5-6 minutes until the pita pockets are warmed through and slightly crispy.

## Servings:

- Makes 2 servings.

# CRISPY AIR FRIED VEGGIE QUESADILLAS

## Ingredients:

- 2 large flour tortillas

- 1 cup shredded cheese (such as Monterey Jack or Mexican blend)

- 1/2 cup diced bell peppers

- 1/4 cup diced onions

- 1/4 cup black beans, drained and rinsed

- 1/4 cup corn kernels (fresh or frozen)

- Guacamole, salsa, and sour cream for serving

## Machine Temperature:

- Preheat your air fryer to 370°F (185°C).

## Time:

- Cook for 4-5 minutes until the tortillas are crispy and the cheese is melted.

## Servings:

- Makes 2 quesadillas.

# CONCLUSION

With these air-fried sandwiches and wraps, you can enjoy a quick and delicious meal without the need for a stovetop or oven. From classic grilled cheese to flavorful falafel pita pockets, your air fryer makes it easy to create satisfying meals with minimal effort. Whether you're cooking for yourself or feeding a crowd, these recipes are sure to become favorites in your kitchen!

In the next chapter, we'll explore some indulgent desserts that you can whip up in your air fryer for a sweet treat anytime. Get ready to satisfy your sweet tooth with these irresistible delights!

# CHAPTER 13

## SIZZLING STEAK RECIPES

In this chapter, we'll explore the art of cooking the perfect steak in your air fryer. From juicy ribeye to tender sirloin, these recipes will take your steak game to the next level with mouthwatering flavors and succulent textures. Get ready to sizzle with these easy and tasty steak recipes!

## JUICY AIR FRYER RIBEYE STEAK

**Ingredients:**

- 2 ribeye steaks, about 1 inch thick

- 2 tablespoons olive oil

- 2 cloves garlic, minced

- Salt and pepper to taste

- Fresh rosemary sprigs for garnish (optional)

**Machine Temperature:**

- Preheat your air fryer to 400°F (200°C).

**Time:**

- Cook for 8-10 minutes for medium-rare or adjust to your desired level of doneness.

**Servings:**

- Serves 2.

# FLAVORFUL AIR FRIED SIRLOIN STEAK BITES

**Ingredients:**

- 1 lb sirloin steak, cut into bite-sized pieces

- 2 tablespoons soy sauce

- 1 tablespoon Worcestershire sauce

- 1 teaspoon garlic powder

- 1 teaspoon smoked paprika

- Salt and pepper to taste

- Fresh parsley for garnish

**Machine Temperature:**

- Preheat your air fryer to 400°F (200°C).

**Time:**

- Cook for 6-8 minutes until steak bites are browned and cooked to your preferred level of doneness.

**Servings:**

- Serves 4.

# CRISPY AIR FRYER STEAK FRIES

**Ingredients:**

- 2 large russet potatoes, cut into wedges

- 2 tablespoons olive oil

- 1 teaspoon garlic powder

- 1 teaspoon paprika

- Salt and pepper to taste

- Fresh parsley for garnish

**Machine Temperature:**

- Preheat your air fryer to 380°F (190°C).

**Time:**

- Cook for 20-25 minutes, shaking the basket halfway through, until steak fries are crispy and golden brown.

**Servings:**

- Serves 4.

# MOUTHWATERING AIR FRIED BEEF KABOBS

**Ingredients:**

- 1 lb beef sirloin, cut into 1-inch cubes

- 1 bell pepper, cut into chunks

- 1 red onion, cut into chunks

- 8 cherry tomatoes

- 2 tablespoons olive oil

- 2 cloves garlic, minced

- 1 teaspoon dried oregano

- Salt and pepper to taste

- Metal or bamboo skewers, soaked in water for 30 minutes

**Machine Temperature:**

- Preheat your air fryer to 380°F (190°C).

**Time:**

- Cook for 10-12 minutes, turning halfway through, until beef is cooked to your preferred level of doneness.

**Servings:**

- Serves 4.

# CONCLUSION

With these sizzling steak recipes, you can enjoy restaurant-quality meals right in the comfort of your own home using your air fryer. Whether you prefer ribeye, sirloin, or beef kabobs, these recipes are sure to impress with their flavor and tenderness. Get ready to elevate your steak game and delight your taste buds with these mouthwatering creations!

In the next chapter, we'll explore some refreshing salads and sides that pair perfectly with your favorite air-fried dishes. Get ready to enjoy a complete and satisfying meal with these delicious accompaniments!

# CHAPTER 14

## POULTRY POWER: TURKEY AND DUCK

In this chapter, we'll explore the delectable world of turkey and duck dishes that are cooked to perfection in your air fryer. From succulent turkey breast to crispy duck legs, these recipes will showcase the versatility and flavor of poultry, making them perfect for any meal occasion.

## AIR FRYER TURKEY BREAST

**Ingredients:**

- 1 turkey breast, boneless, approximately 2-3 lbs

- 2 tablespoons olive oil

- 1 teaspoon dried thyme

- 1 teaspoon dried rosemary

- Salt and pepper to taste

**Machine Temperature:**

- Preheat your air fryer to 350°F (175°C).

**Time:**

- Cook for 25-30 minutes, until the internal temperature reaches 165°F (74°C).

**Serving:**

- Serves 4-6.

# CRISPY DUCK LEGS WITH ORANGE GLAZE

**Ingredients:**

- 4 duck legs

- 1/4 cup orange juice

- 2 tablespoons soy sauce

- 2 tablespoons honey

- 1 tablespoon rice vinegar

- 1 teaspoon grated ginger

- Salt and pepper to taste

**Machine Temperature:**

- Preheat your air fryer to 400°F (200°C).

**Time:**

- Cook for 30-35 minutes, until the skin is crispy and the internal temperature reaches 165°F (74°C).

**Serving:**

- Serves 2-4.

# TURKEY MEATBALLS IN MARINARA SAUCE

**Ingredients:**

- 1 lb ground turkey

- 1/2 cup breadcrumbs

- 1/4 cup grated Parmesan cheese

- 1 egg

- 2 cloves garlic, minced

- 1 teaspoon dried oregano

- Salt and pepper to taste

- 2 cups marinara sauce

**Machine Temperature:**

- Preheat your air fryer to 380°F (190°C).

**Time:**

- Cook for 12-15 minutes, until meatballs are cooked through.

**Serving:**

- Makes about 20 meatballs.

# DUCK BREAST WITH CHERRY SAUCE

**Ingredients:**

- 2 duck breasts

- Salt and pepper to taste

- 1 cup fresh or frozen cherries, pitted

- 2 tablespoons balsamic vinegar

- 2 tablespoons honey

- 1/4 cup chicken broth

**Machine Temperature:**

- Preheat your air fryer to 380°F (190°C).

**Time:**

- Cook for 15-18 minutes, until duck breast is cooked to your desired level of doneness.

**Serving:**

- Serves 2.

# CONCLUSION

With these poultry power recipes featuring turkey and duck, you'll discover a whole new level of flavor and convenience with your air fryer. Whether you're cooking for a special occasion or a weeknight dinner, these recipes are sure to impress. Enjoy the magic of poultry with these mouthwatering dishes!

# CHAPTER 15

## INTERNATIONAL FLAVORS: ASIAN-INSPIRED DISHES

Embark on a culinary journey through the vibrant flavors of Asia with these tantalizing dishes, all prepared effortlessly in your air fryer. From savory stir-fries to crispy spring rolls, these recipes will bring the taste of the Far East right into your kitchen. Get ready to explore the delicious world of Asian-inspired cuisine with these easy and flavorful recipes!

## CRISPY AIR FRYER ORANGE CHICKEN

**Ingredients:**

- 1 lb boneless, skinless chicken breast, cut into bite-sized pieces

- 1/2 cup cornstarch

- 2 eggs, beaten

- 1 tablespoon vegetable oil

- 1/2 cup orange marmalade

- 2 tablespoons soy sauce

- 1 tablespoon rice vinegar

- 1 teaspoon sesame oil

- 1 teaspoon grated ginger

- 2 cloves garlic, minced

- Sesame seeds and sliced green onions for garnish

**Machine Temperature:**

- Preheat your air fryer to 380°F (190°C).

**Time:**

- Cook for 12-15 minutes, shaking the basket halfway through, until chicken is crispy and cooked through.

**Serving:**

- Serves 4.

# FLAVORFUL AIR FRIED VEGETABLE SPRING ROLLS

**Ingredients:**

- 8 spring roll wrappers

- 2 cups shredded cabbage

- 1 carrot, julienned

- 1/2 cup bean sprouts

- 2 green onions, thinly sliced

- 2 tablespoons soy sauce

- 1 tablespoon sesame oil

- 1 teaspoon grated ginger

- 1 teaspoon garlic powder

- Sweet chili sauce for dipping

**Machine Temperature:**

- Preheat your air fryer to 370°F (185°C).

**Time:**

- Cook for 10-12 minutes, until spring rolls are golden and crispy.

**Serving:**

- Makes 8 spring rolls.

# CRISPY AIR FRYER TERIYAKI TOFU

**Ingredients:**

- 1 block extra-firm tofu, pressed and cubed

- 1/4 cup soy sauce

- 2 tablespoons honey

- 1 tablespoon rice vinegar

- 1 teaspoon sesame oil

- 1 teaspoon grated ginger

- 2 cloves garlic, minced

- Sesame seeds and sliced green onions for garnish

**Machine Temperature:**

- Preheat your air fryer to 400°F (200°C).

**Time:**

- Cook for 15-20 minutes, shaking the basket halfway through, until tofu is crispy and golden.

**Serving:**

- Serves 2-3.

# FLAVORFUL AIR FRIED ASIAN VEGETABLE STIR-FRY

**Ingredients:**

- 2 cups mixed vegetables (such as bell peppers, broccoli, snap peas, carrots)

- 2 tablespoons soy sauce

- 1 tablespoon hoisin sauce

- 1 tablespoon oyster sauce

- 1 tablespoon vegetable oil

- 1 teaspoon grated ginger

- 2 cloves garlic, minced

- Cooked rice or noodles for serving

**Machine Temperature:**

- Preheat your air fryer to 380°F (190°C).

**Time:**

- Cook for 8-10 minutes, tossing halfway through, until vegetables are tender-crisp.

**Serving:**

- Serves 2-3.

# CONCLUSION

Transport your taste buds to Asia with these irresistible Asian-inspired dishes cooked to perfection in your air fryer. Whether you're craving the sweet and tangy flavors of orange chicken, the crispy goodness of vegetable spring rolls, or the savory delight of teriyaki tofu, these recipes are sure to satisfy. Enjoy the bold and delicious flavors of Asia with these easy and tasty recipes!

In the next chapter, we'll explore the comforting and hearty flavors of Mediterranean cuisine, bringing a taste of the Mediterranean right into your home with your air fryer. Get ready for a culinary adventure filled with delicious dishes and unforgettable flavors!

# CHAPTER 16

## MEDITERRANEAN MAGIC

Indulge in the rich and vibrant flavors of the Mediterranean with these mouthwatering recipes designed to transport your taste buds to the sun-soaked shores of Greece, Italy, and beyond. From crispy falafel to succulent kebabs, these dishes capture the essence of Mediterranean cuisine and are perfectly suited for preparation in your air fryer. Prepare to embark on a culinary journey filled with Mediterranean magic!

## CRISPY AIR FRYER FALAFEL

**Ingredients:**

- 1 can chickpeas, drained and rinsed

- 1/2 onion, chopped

- 2 cloves garlic, minced

- 1/4 cup fresh parsley, chopped

- 1 teaspoon ground cumin

- 1 teaspoon ground coriander

- 1/2 teaspoon baking powder

- Salt and pepper to taste

- 2 tablespoons all-purpose flour

- Olive oil cooking spray

**Machine Temperature:**

- Preheat your air fryer to 370°F (185°C).

**Time:**

- Cook for 12-15 minutes, flipping halfway through, until falafel is golden and crispy.

**Serving:**

- Makes about 12 falafel balls.

# FLAVORFUL AIR FRIED GREEK CHICKEN KEBABS

**Ingredients:**

- 1 lb chicken breast, cut into cubes

- 1/4 cup Greek yogurt

- 2 tablespoons olive oil

- 1 tablespoon lemon juice

- 2 cloves garlic, minced

- 1 teaspoon dried oregano

- Salt and pepper to taste

- Cherry tomatoes, red onion slices, and bell pepper chunks for skewering

**Machine Temperature:**

- Preheat your air fryer to 380°F (190°C).

**Time:**

- Cook for 10-12 minutes, turning halfway through, until chicken is cooked through.

**Serving:**

- Serves 2-3.

# CRISPY AIR FRIED EGGPLANT PARMESAN

**Ingredients:**

- 1 large eggplant, sliced into rounds

- 1 cup breadcrumbs

- 1/2 cup grated Parmesan cheese

- 1 teaspoon dried oregano

- 1 teaspoon dried basil

- Salt and pepper to taste

- Marinara sauce

- Mozzarella cheese slices

**Machine Temperature:**

- Preheat your air fryer to 380°F (190°C).

**Time:**

- Cook for 12-15 minutes until eggplant is tender and coating is crispy.

**Serving:**

- Serves 2-4.

# MEDITERRANEAN ROASTED VEGETABLE PLATTER

**Ingredients:**

- 1 zucchini, sliced

- 1 yellow squash, sliced

- 1 red bell pepper, sliced

- 1 red onion, sliced

- 1 tablespoon olive oil

- 1 teaspoon dried oregano

- 1 teaspoon dried thyme

- Salt and pepper to taste

- Hummus and pita bread for serving

**Machine Temperature:**

- Preheat your air fryer to 380°F (190°C).

**Time:**

- Cook for 15-20 minutes, tossing halfway through, until vegetables are tender and slightly charred.

**Serving:**

- Serves 4.

# CONCLUSION

Experience the enchanting flavors of the Mediterranean with these delectable recipes that bring the essence of the region straight to your plate. Whether you're savoring crispy falafel, indulging in Greek chicken kebabs, enjoying eggplant Parmesan, or feasting on a roasted vegetable platter, your air fryer will help you achieve Mediterranean magic in every bite. Get ready to delight in the flavors of the Mediterranean with these easy and tasty recipes!

# CHAPTER 17

## LATIN AMERICAN FAVORITES

In this chapter, we'll dive into the vibrant and flavorful world of Latin American cuisine, showcasing beloved dishes from across the region that are perfect for your air fryer. From crispy empanadas to zesty tacos, these recipes will transport you to the streets of Latin America with every bite. Get ready to savor the bold and irresistible flavors of Latin American favorites!

## CRISPY AIR FRYER EMPANADAS

**Ingredients:**

- 1 package of pre-made empanada dough (or homemade dough)

- 1 cup cooked ground beef or shredded chicken

- 1/2 cup diced onions

- 1/2 cup diced bell peppers

- 1/2 cup diced tomatoes

- 1 teaspoon ground cumin

- 1 teaspoon smoked paprika

- Salt and pepper to taste

- 1 egg, beaten (for egg wash)

**Machine Temperature:**

- Preheat your air fryer to 375°F (190°C).

**Time:**

- Cook for 12-15 minutes until empanadas are golden and crispy.

**Serving:**

- Makes 8 empanadas.

# FLAVORFUL AIR FRIED CHICKEN TACOS

**Ingredients:**

- 1 lb chicken breast, sliced into strips

- 2 tablespoons taco seasoning

- 1 tablespoon vegetable oil

- 8 small corn or flour tortillas

- 1 cup shredded lettuce

- 1/2 cup diced tomatoes

- 1/2 cup diced onions

- 1/4 cup chopped cilantro

- Lime wedges for serving

- Salsa and sour cream for topping

**Machine Temperature:**

- Preheat your air fryer to 400°F (200°C).

**Time:**

- Cook for 8-10 minutes until chicken is cooked through and slightly charred.

**Serving:**

- Serves 4.

# CRISPY AIR FRYER PLANTAIN CHIPS

**Ingredients:**

- 2 ripe plantains

- 2 tablespoons olive oil

- Salt to taste

**Machine Temperature:**

- Preheat your air fryer to 380°F (190°C).

**Time:**

- Cook for 8-10 minutes until plantain chips are crispy and golden brown.

**Serving:**

- Serves 2-4.

# FLAVORFUL AIR FRIED BLACK BEAN TAQUITOS

**Ingredients:**

- 1 can black beans, drained and rinsed

- 1/2 cup diced onions

- 1/2 cup diced bell peppers

- 1 teaspoon ground cumin

- 1 teaspoon chili powder

- Salt and pepper to taste

- 8 small corn tortillas

- Guacamole, salsa, and sour cream for serving

**Machine Temperature:**

- Preheat your air fryer to 375°F (190°C).

**Time:**

- Cook for 10-12 minutes until taquitos are crispy and golden.

**Serving:**

- Serves 4.

# CONCLUSION

With these Latin American favorites cooked to perfection in your air fryer, you can enjoy the bold and vibrant flavors of the region right in your own home. Whether you're indulging in crispy empanadas, zesty chicken tacos, or crunchy plantain chips, these recipes are sure to become family favorites. Get ready to spice up your mealtime with these delicious Latin American dishes!

In the next chapter, we'll explore some delectable desserts that you can easily prepare in your air fryer for a sweet ending to any meal. Get ready to satisfy your sweet tooth with these irresistible treats!

# CHAPTER 18

## INDIAN INFUSIONS

Indulge in the rich and aromatic flavors of Indian cuisine with these delightful recipes tailored for your air fryer. From crispy pakoras to tender tandoori chicken, these dishes will transport you to the bustling streets of India with every bite. Get ready to experience the magic of Indian spices and ingredients with these easy and delicious recipes!

# CRISPY AIR FRYER VEGETABLE PAKORAS

**Ingredients:**

- 1 cup chickpea flour (besan)

- 1/4 cup rice flour

- 1/2 cup water

- 1 cup mixed vegetables (such as potatoes, onions, cauliflower, spinach), finely chopped

- 1 teaspoon cumin seeds

- 1 teaspoon coriander powder

- 1/2 teaspoon turmeric powder

- 1/2 teaspoon red chili powder

- Salt to taste

- Fresh cilantro leaves, chopped

- Mint chutney or tamarind chutney for serving

**Machine Temperature:**

- Preheat your air fryer to 380°F (190°C).

**Time:**

- Cook for 10-12 minutes until pakoras are golden and crispy.

**Serving:**

- Makes about 12 pakoras.

# FLAVORFUL AIR FRIED TANDOORI CHICKEN

**Ingredients:**

- 4 chicken thighs, skinless and boneless

- 1/2 cup plain yogurt

- 2 tablespoons tandoori masala

- 1 tablespoon lemon juice

- 1 teaspoon grated ginger

- 1 teaspoon grated garlic

- Salt to taste

- Fresh cilantro leaves for garnish

- Lemon wedges for serving

**Machine Temperature:**

- Preheat your air fryer to 375°F (190°C).

**Time:**

- Cook for 20-25 minutes until chicken is cooked through and slightly charred.

**Serving:**

- Serves 2-4.

# CRISPY AIR FRYER SAMOSAS

**Ingredients:**

- 1 cup mashed potatoes

- 1/2 cup green peas, boiled

- 1/4 cup finely chopped onions

- 1 green chili, finely chopped

- 1 teaspoon cumin seeds

- 1 teaspoon

- 1/2 teaspoon turmeric powder

- Salt to taste

- 12 samosa pastry sheets (store-bought or homemade)

- 2 tablespoons vegetable oil

- Mint chutney or tamarind chutney for serving

## Machine Temperature:

- Preheat your air fryer to 380°F (190°C).

## Time:

- Cook for 10-12 minutes until samosas are golden and crispy.

## Serving:

- Makes 12 samosas.

# FLAVORFUL AIR FRIED PANEER TIKKA

## Ingredients:

- 1 block paneer, cut into cubes

- 1/2 cup plain yogurt

- 2 tablespoons tikka masala

- 1 tablespoon lemon juice

- 1 teaspoon grated ginger

- 1 teaspoon grated garlic

- Salt to taste

- Onion slices and bell pepper slices for skewering

- Fresh cilantro leaves for garnish

- Lemon wedges for serving

**Machine Temperature:**

- Preheat your air fryer to 380°F (190°C).

**Time:**

- Cook for 12-15 minutes until paneer is golden and slightly charred.

**Serving:**

- Serves 2-3.

# CONCLUSION

With these Indian-inspired recipes cooked to perfection in your air fryer, you can savor the exotic flavors and spices of India right in your own home. Whether you're enjoying crispy vegetable pakoras, succulent tandoori chicken, savory samosas, or flavorful paneer tikka, these dishes are sure to delight your taste buds and impress your family and friends. Get ready to embark on a culinary journey through the vibrant and diverse flavors of India with these easy and tasty recipes!

In the next chapter, we'll explore some comforting and hearty dishes perfect for cozy family dinners. Get ready to enjoy satisfying meals with your air fryer!

# CHAPTER 19

## MIDDLE EASTERN DELIGHTS

Transport your taste buds to the enchanting world of Middle Eastern cuisine with these mouthwatering recipes crafted specifically for your air fryer. From crispy falafel to succulent kebabs, these dishes will evoke the flavors and aromas of the region right in your own kitchen. Get ready to embark on a culinary journey through the Middle East with these easy and flavorful recipes!

## CRISPY AIR FRYER FALAFEL

**Ingredients:**

- 1 cup dried chickpeas, soaked overnight

- 1/2 onion, chopped

- 2 cloves garlic, minced

- 1/4 cup fresh parsley, chopped

- 1/4 cup fresh cilantro, chopped

- 1 teaspoon ground cumin

- 1 teaspoon ground coriander

- 1/2 teaspoon baking powder

- Salt and pepper to taste

- Olive oil for spraying

**Machine Temperature:**

- Preheat your air fryer to 375°F (190°C).

**Time:**

- Cook for 12-15 minutes until falafel are golden and crispy.

**Serving:**

- Makes about 16 falafel.

# FLAVORFUL AIR FRIED CHICKEN SHAWAMAR

**Ingredients:**

- 1 lb boneless, skinless chicken thighs

- 2 tablespoons olive oil

- 2 cloves garlic, minced

- 1 teaspoon ground cumin

- 1 teaspoon ground paprika

- 1/2 teaspoon ground turmeric

- 1/2 teaspoon ground cinnamon

- Salt and pepper to taste

- Pita bread, lettuce, tomatoes, and tahini sauce for serving

## Machine Temperature:

- Preheat your air fryer to 375°F (190°C).

## Time:

- Cook for 15-18 minutes until chicken is cooked through and slightly charred.

## Serving:

- Serves 4.

# CRISPY AIR FRYER STUFFED GRAPE LEAVES (DOLMAS)

## Ingredients:

- 1 jar grape leaves, drained and rinsed

- 1 cup cooked rice

- 1/2 cup chopped fresh parsley

- 1/4 cup chopped fresh dill

- 1/4 cup chopped fresh mint

- 1/4 cup pine nuts, toasted

- 1/4 cup lemon juice

- 2 tablespoons olive oil

- Salt and pepper to taste

## Machine Temperature:

- Preheat your air fryer to 375°F (190°C).

## Time:

- Cook for 8-10 minutes until grape leaves are crispy.

## Serving:

- Makes about 20 stuffed grape leaves.

# FLAVORFUL AIR-FRIED LAMB KOFTA KEBABS

## Ingredients:

- 1 lb ground lamb

- 1/2 onion, grated

- 2 cloves garlic, minced

- 1/4 cup chopped fresh parsley

- 1 teaspoon ground cumin

- 1 teaspoon ground coriander

- 1/2 teaspoon ground paprika

- Salt and pepper to taste

- Skewers

- Tzatziki sauce for serving

## Machine Temperature:

- Preheat your air fryer to 375°F (190°C).

## Time:

- Cook for 12-15 minutes until kebabs are cooked through and slightly charred.

**Serving:**

- Serves 4.

## CONCLUSION

With these Middle Eastern delights cooked to perfection in your air fryer, you can experience the exotic flavors and aromas of the region from the comfort of your own home. Whether you're indulging in crispy falafel, flavorful chicken shawarma, stuffed grape leaves, or succulent lamb kofta kebabs, these recipes are sure to impress. Get ready to enjoy the rich and diverse cuisine of the Middle East with these easy and tasty recipes!

# CHAPTER 20

## COMFORT FOOD CLASSICS

Indulge in the timeless and comforting flavors of classic comfort foods, reinvented for your air fryer. From crispy chicken tenders to gooey grilled cheese sandwiches, these recipes will warm your soul and satisfy your cravings. Get ready to experience the magic of comfort food classics with the convenience of your air fryer!

# CRISPY AIR FRYER CHICKEN TENDERS

**Ingredients:**

- 1 lb chicken tenders

- 1 cup breadcrumbs

- 1/2 cup grated Parmesan cheese

- 1 teaspoon garlic powder

- 1 teaspoon paprika

- Salt and pepper to taste

- 2 eggs, beaten

**Machine Temperature:**

- Preheat your air fryer to 400°F (200°C).

**Time:**

- Cook for 10-12 minutes, flipping halfway through, until chicken is golden and crispy.

**Serving:**

- Serves 4.

# FLAVORFUL AIR FRIED MACARONI AND CHEESE BITES

**Ingredients:**

- 2 cups cooked macaroni noodles

- 1 cup shredded cheddar cheese

- 1/4 cup grated Parmesan cheese

- 1/4 cup milk

- 1 egg

- 1/2 cup breadcrumbs

- Salt and pepper to taste

**Machine Temperature:**

- Preheat your air fryer to 370°F (185°C).

**Time:**

- Cook for 8-10 minutes until mac and cheese bites are golden and crispy.

**Serving:**

- Makes about 12 bites.

# CRISPY AIR FRYER FRENCH FRIES

**Ingredients:**

- 2 large potatoes, cut into fries

- 2 tablespoons olive oil

- 1 teaspoon garlic powder

- 1 teaspoon paprika

- Salt and pepper to taste

**Machine Temperature:**

- Preheat your air fryer to 380°F (190°C).

**Time:**

- Cook for 15-20 minutes, shaking the basket halfway through, until fries are golden and crispy.

**Serving:**

- Serves 2-3.

# FLAVORFUL AIR FRIED GRILLED CHEESE SANDWICHES

**Ingredients:**

- 4 slices bread

- 4 slices cheddar cheese

- 2 tablespoons butter, softened

**Machine Temperature:**

- Preheat your air fryer to 360°F (180°C).

**Time:**

- Cook for 4-5 minutes, flipping halfway through, until bread is golden and cheese is melted.

**Serving:**

- Serves 2.

# CONCLUSION

With these comfort food classics reinvented for your air fryer, you can enjoy all the flavors and nostalgia of your favorite dishes with a healthier twist. Whether you're craving crispy chicken tenders, cheesy mac and cheese bites, perfectly seasoned french fries, or gooey grilled cheese sandwiches, these recipes are sure to bring warmth and satisfaction to your table. Get ready to indulge in the ultimate comfort food experience with these easy and tasty recipes!

# CHAPTER 21

## POTATOES GALORE: FRIES, CHIPS, AND MORE

Potatoes are one of the most versatile ingredients, and with your air fryer, you can easily transform them into crispy fries, crunchy chips, and so much more. In this chapter, we'll explore the endless possibilities of potato dishes that you can create with your air fryer. Get ready to enjoy the ultimate comfort food with these easy and delicious potato recipes!

# CRISPY AIR FRYER FRENCH FRIES

**Ingredients:**

- 2 large potatoes, cut into fries

- 2 tablespoons olive oil

- 1 teaspoon garlic powder

- 1 teaspoon paprika

- Salt and pepper to taste

**Machine Temperature:**

- Preheat your air fryer to 380°F (190°C).

**Time:**

- Cook for 15-20 minutes, shaking the basket halfway through, until fries are golden and crispy.

**Serving:**

- Serves 2-3.

# FLAVORFUL AIR FRIED POTATO CHIPS

**Ingredients:**

- 2 large potatoes, thinly sliced

- 2 tablespoons olive oil

- 1 teaspoon salt

- 1/2 teaspoon black pepper

- 1/2 teaspoon paprika

**Machine Temperature:**

- Preheat your air fryer to 360°F (180°C).

**Time:**

- Cook for 10-12 minutes until chips are golden and crispy.

**Serving:**

- Serves 2-3.

# CRISPY AIR FRYER POTATO WEDGES

**Ingredients:**

- 2 large potatoes, cut into wedges

- 2 tablespoons olive oil

- 1 teaspoon garlic powder

- 1 teaspoon onion powder

- 1 teaspoon paprika

- Salt and pepper to taste

**Machine Temperature:**

- Preheat your air fryer to 400°F (200°C).

**Time:**

- Cook for 20-25 minutes, flipping halfway through, until wedges are golden and crispy.

**Serving:**

- Serves 2-4.

# FLAVORFUL AIR FRIED LOADED POTATO SKINS

**Ingredients:**

- 4 large russet potatoes

- 2 tablespoons olive oil

- Salt and pepper to taste

- 1 cup shredded cheddar cheese

- 4 slices bacon, cooked and crumbled

- 2 green onions, chopped

- Sour cream for serving

**Machine Temperature:**

- Preheat your air fryer to 400°F (200°C).

**Time:**

- Cook for 30-35 minutes until potatoes are tender.

**Serving:**

- Serves 4.

# CONCLUSION

With these potato recipes for your air fryer, you can enjoy the crispy and delicious flavors of fries, chips, wedges, and loaded potato skins right in the comfort of your own home. Whether you're craving a classic side dish or a satisfying snack, these recipes are sure to please. Get ready to indulge in the irresistible taste of potatoes galore with your air fryer!

# CHAPTER 22

## CREATIVE CAULIFLOWER CREATIONS

Cauliflower is a versatile and nutritious vegetable that can be transformed into a variety of delicious dishes with the help of your air fryer. In this chapter, we'll explore creative and flavorful cauliflower recipes that are easy to make and perfect for any meal occasion. Get ready to elevate your culinary game with these innovative cauliflower creations!

## CRISPY AIR FRYER CAULIFLOWER BITES

**Ingredients:**

- 1 head cauliflower, cut into florets

- 1/2 cup all-purpose flour

- 1/2 cup milk (or plant-based milk)

- 1 teaspoon garlic powder

- 1 teaspoon paprika

- Salt and pepper to taste

- Cooking spray

**Machine Temperature:**

- Preheat your air fryer to 375°F (190°C).

**Time:**

- Cook for 15-18 minutes, shaking the basket halfway through, until cauliflower is golden and crispy.

**Serving:**

- Serves 4-6.

# FLAVORFUL AIR FRIED CAULIFLOWER STEAKS

**Ingredients:**

- 1 large cauliflower head

- 2 tablespoons olive oil

- 1 teaspoon garlic powder

- 1 teaspoon smoked paprika

- Salt and pepper to taste

**Machine Temperature:**

- Preheat your air fryer to 380°F (190°C).

**Time:**

- Cook for 12-15 minutes, flipping halfway through, until cauliflower steaks are tender and golden.

**Serving:**

- Serves 2-3.

# CRISPY AIR FRYER CAULIFLOWER TOTS

**Ingredients:**

- 2 cups cauliflower rice (fresh or frozen)

- 1/2 cup breadcrumbs

- 1/4 cup grated Parmesan cheese

- 1 egg, beaten

- 1 teaspoon garlic powder

- 1 teaspoon onion powder

- Salt and pepper to taste

**Machine Temperature:**

- Preheat your air fryer to 375°F (190°C).

**Time:**

- Cook for 10-12 minutes, flipping halfway through, until tots are golden and crispy.

**Serving:**

- Makes about 20 tots.

# FLAVORFUL AIR FRIED BUFFALO CAULIFLOWER WINGS

**Ingredients:**

- 1 head cauliflower, cut into florets

- 1/2 cup all-purpose flour

- 1/2 cup water

- 1 teaspoon garlic powder

- 1 teaspoon paprika

- 1/2 cup buffalo sauce

- 2 tablespoons melted butter (or vegan butter)

- Salt and pepper to taste

- Ranch or blue cheese dressing for serving

**Machine Temperature:**

- Preheat your air fryer to 380°F (190°C).

**Time:**

- Cook for 15-18 minutes, shaking the basket halfway through, until cauliflower is crispy and sauce is caramelized.

Serving:

- Serves 4-6.

# CONCLUSION

With these creative cauliflower recipes for your air fryer, you can enjoy the versatility and deliciousness of this nutritious vegetable in a whole new way. Whether you're craving crispy cauliflower bites, flavorful cauliflower steaks, crunchy cauliflower tots, or spicy buffalo cauliflower wings, these recipes are sure to satisfy. Get ready to impress your family and friends with these tasty cauliflower creations!

# CHAPTER 23

## AIR-FRIED PASTA PERFECTION

Pasta lovers, rejoice! In this chapter, we'll explore how your air fryer can elevate pasta dishes to new heights, delivering perfectly cooked noodles with crispy edges and deliciously infused flavors. From classic favorites to inventive twists, these air-fried pasta recipes are sure to become staples in your kitchen. Get ready to experience pasta perfection like never before!

## CRISPY AIR FRYER RAVIOLI

**Ingredients:**

- 1 package refrigerated ravioli (any flavor)

- 1 cup breadcrumbs

- 1/2 cup grated Parmesan cheese

- 2 eggs, beaten

- 1 teaspoon Italian seasoning

- Marinara sauce for serving

**Machine Temperature:**

- Preheat your air fryer to 380°F (190°C).

**Time:**

- Cook for 8-10 minutes until ravioli is golden and crispy.

**Serving:**

- Serves 4.

# FLAVORFUL AIR FRIED SPAGHETTI AND MEATBALLS

**Ingredients:**

- 8 oz spaghetti noodles, cooked al dente

- 1 cup marinara sauce

- 1/2 cup grated Parmesan cheese

- 1/4 cup chopped fresh basil

- 12 cooked meatballs

- Salt and pepper to taste

**Machine Temperature:**

- Preheat your air fryer to 375°F (190°C).

**Time:**

- Cook for 10-12 minutes until meatballs are heated through and spaghetti is crispy.

**Serving:**

- Serves 2-3.

# CRISPY AIR FRYER MAC AND CHEESE BALLS

**Ingredients:**

- 2 cups leftover macaroni and cheese, chilled

- 1 cup breadcrumbs

- 1/2 cup grated cheddar cheese

- 2 eggs, beaten

- Salt and pepper to taste

- Ketchup or ranch dressing for dipping

**Machine Temperature:**

- Preheat your air fryer to 380°F (190°C).

**Time:**

- Cook for 10-12 minutes until mac and cheese balls are golden and crispy.

**Serving:**

- Serves 4-6.

# FLAVORFUL AIR FRIED LASAGNA ROLLS

**Ingredients:**

- 8 lasagna noodles, cooked

- 1 cup ricotta cheese

- 1 cup marinara sauce

- 1/2 cup shredded mozzarella cheese

- 1/4 cup grated Parmesan cheese

- Fresh basil leaves for garnish

- Salt and pepper to taste

**Machine Temperature:**

- Preheat your air fryer to 375°F (190°C).

**Time:**

- Cook for 12-15 minutes until lasagna rolls are heated through and cheese is melted.

-Serves 2-4.

# CONCLUSION

With these air-fried pasta recipes, you can enjoy the comforting flavors of your favorite Italian dishes with a crispy twist. Whether you're indulging in crispy ravioli, savory spaghetti and meatballs, cheesy mac and cheese balls, or flavorful lasagna rolls, these recipes are sure to satisfy your pasta cravings. Get ready to experience pasta perfection with your air fryer!

# CHAPTER 24

## RICE AND GRAIN INNOVATIONS

In this chapter, we'll explore the versatility of your air fryer when it comes to cooking rice and grains. From crispy fried rice to flavorful grain bowls, these recipes will show you how to achieve perfectly cooked and deliciously seasoned rice and grains using your air fryer. Get ready to revolutionize the way you prepare these pantry staples with these innovative and tasty recipes!

## CRISPY AIR FRYER FRIED RICE

**Ingredients:**

- 2 cups cooked rice (preferably day-old)

- 2 eggs, beaten

- 1 cup mixed vegetables (such as peas, carrots, and bell peppers)

- 1/4 cup diced onions

- 2 cloves garlic, minced

- 2 tablespoons soy sauce

- 1 tablespoon sesame oil

- Salt and pepper to taste

- Green onions for garnish

**Machine Temperature:**

- Preheat your air fryer to 370°F (185°C).

**Time:**

- Cook for 10-12 minutes, stirring occasionally, until rice is crispy and vegetables are tender.

**Serving:**

- Serves 2-3.

# FLAVORFUL AIR FRIED QUINOA SALAD

**Ingredients:**

- 1 cup quinoa, rinsed

- 2 cups water or vegetable broth

- 1 cup cherry tomatoes, halved

- 1 cucumber, diced

- 1/4 cup chopped fresh parsley

- 1/4 cup chopped fresh mint

- 2 tablespoons olive oil

- 1 tablespoon lemon juice

- Salt and pepper to taste

- Feta cheese for topping (optional)

**Machine Temperature:**

- Preheat your air fryer to 360°F (180°C).

**Time:**

- Cook for 12-15 minutes until quinoa is fluffy and slightly crispy.

**Serving:**

- Serves 4-6.

# CRISPY AIR FRYER RISOTTO BALLS

## Ingredients:

- 2 cups cooked risotto, chilled

- 1/2 cup grated Parmesan cheese

- 1/4 cup breadcrumbs

- 2 eggs, beaten

- Salt and pepper to taste

- Marinara sauce for dipping

## Machine Temperature:

- Preheat your air fryer to 380°F (190°C).

## Time:

- Cook for 10-12 minutes until risotto balls are golden and crispy.

## Serving:

- Serves 4-6.

# FLAVORFUL AIR FRIED COUSCOUS STUFFED PEPPERS

**Ingredients:**

- 4 bell peppers, halved and seeded

- 1 cup couscous, cooked

- 1/2 cup cooked chickpeas

- 1/4 cup diced tomatoes

- 1/4 cup chopped fresh parsley

- 2 tablespoons olive oil

- 1 tablespoon lemon juice

- 1 teaspoon ground cumin

- Salt and pepper to taste

**Machine Temperature:**

- Preheat your air fryer to 370°F (185°C).

**Time:**

- Cook for 15-18 minutes until peppers are tender and couscous is heated through.

Serving:

- Serves 4.

# CONCLUSION

With these rice and grain innovations for your air fryer, you can enjoy perfectly cooked and flavorful dishes in no time. Whether you're craving crispy fried rice, refreshing quinoa salad, indulgent risotto balls, or wholesome stuffed peppers, these recipes are sure to impress. Get ready to elevate your rice and grain game with the magic of your air fryer!

# CHAPTER 25

## QUICK AND EASY ONE-POT MEALS

In this chapter, we'll explore the convenience of preparing delicious and satisfying one-pot meals using your air fryer. From hearty stews to flavorful pasta dishes, these recipes require minimal preparation and cleanup while delivering maximum flavor. Get ready to simplify your mealtime routine with these quick and easy one-pot wonders!

## FLAVORFUL AIR FRYER CHICKEN AND VEGETABLE STIR FRY

Ingredients:

- 1 lb boneless, skinless chicken breast, sliced

- 2 cups mixed vegetables (such as bell peppers, broccoli, carrots)

- 1/4 cup soy sauce

- 2 tablespoons honey

- 2 cloves garlic, minced

- 1 tablespoon grated ginger

- 2 tablespoons olive oil

- Salt and pepper to taste

- Cooked rice for serving

**Machine Temperature:**

- Preheat your air fryer to 370°F (185°C).

**Time:**

- Cook for 15-18 minutes, stirring halfway through, until chicken is cooked through and vegetables are tender.

**Serving:**

- Serves 4.

# CRISPY AIR FRIED SAUSAGE AND POTATO HASH

**Ingredients:**

- 1 lb smoked sausage, sliced

- 4 cups diced potatoes

- 1 onion, diced

- 1 bell pepper, diced

- 2 tablespoons olive oil

- 1 teaspoon paprika

- 1 teaspoon garlic powder

- Salt and pepper to taste

- Chopped fresh parsley for garnish

**Machine Temperature:**

- Preheat your air fryer to 380°F (190°C).

**Time:**

- Cook for 20-25 minutes, stirring occasionally, until sausage is crispy and potatoes are tender.

**Serving:**

- Serves 4-6.

## FLAVORFUL AIR FRYER JAMBALAYA

**Ingredients:**

- 1 lb shrimp, peeled and deveined

- 1 lb smoked sausage, sliced

- 1 onion, diced

- 1 bell pepper, diced

- 2 stalks celery, diced

- 2 cloves garlic, minced

- 1 cup long-grain rice

- 1 can (14.5 oz) diced tomatoes

- 1 cup chicken broth

- 1 teaspoon Cajun seasoning

- Salt and pepper to taste

- Chopped fresh parsley for garnish

**Machine Temperature:**

- Preheat your air fryer to 370°F (185°C).

**Time:**

- Cook for 20-25 minutes, stirring halfway through, until rice is cooked through and liquid is absorbed.

**Serving:**

- Serves 4-6.

# CONCLUSION

With these quick and easy one-pot meals made in

your air fryer, you can enjoy delicious and satisfying dishes with minimal effort. Whether you're craving a chicken stir-fry, a sausage and potato hash, or a flavorful jambalaya, these recipes are perfect for busy weeknights or lazy weekends. Get ready to simplify your cooking routine and enjoy tasty meals with your air fryer!

# CHAPTER 26

## SWEET TREATS: DESSERTS AND PASTRIES

Indulge your sweet tooth with these delectable desserts and pastries that are perfectly suited for your air fryer. From crispy churros to gooey brownies, these recipes will satisfy any craving and impress your friends and family. Get ready to elevate your dessert game with these easy and irresistible sweet treats!

# CRISPY AIR FRYER CHURROS

**Ingredients:**

- 1 cup water

- 1/2 cup unsalted butter

- 2 tablespoons granulated sugar

- 1/4 teaspoon salt

- 1 cup all-purpose flour

- 2 eggs

- 1 teaspoon vanilla extract

- 1/4 cup granulated sugar mixed with 1 teaspoon ground cinnamon (for coating)

- Chocolate sauce or caramel sauce for dipping

**Machine Temperature:**

- Preheat your air fryer to 375°F (190°C).

**Time:**

- Cook for 8-10 minutes until churros are golden brown and crispy.

**Serving:**

- Makes about 12 churros.

Flavorful Air Fried Apple Hand Pies

## Ingredients:

- 2 sheets store-bought pie crust

- 2 cups diced apples

- 1/4 cup granulated sugar

- 1 teaspoon ground cinnamon

- 1 tablespoon lemon juice

- 1 egg, beaten (for egg wash)

- Powdered sugar for dusting

## Machine Temperature:

- Preheat your air fryer to 370°F (185°C).

## Time:

- Cook for 12-15 minutes until pies are golden and filling is bubbly.

## Serving:

- Makes about 6 hand pies.

# CRISPY AIR FRYER DONUTS

**Ingredients:**

- 1 can (16 oz) refrigerated biscuit dough

- 1 cup powdered sugar

- 2 tablespoons milk

- 1/2 teaspoon vanilla extract

- Sprinkles or cinnamon sugar for coating

**Machine Temperature:**

- Preheat your air fryer to 350°F (175°C).

**Time:**

- Cook for 4-6 minutes until donuts are golden brown.

**Serving:**

- Makes about 8 donuts.

# FLAVORFUL AIR FRIED BROWNIES

**Ingredients:**

- 1 box brownie mix

- Ingredients listed on the brownie mix box (usually eggs, oil, and water)

- 1/2 cup chocolate chips (optional)

**Machine Temperature:**

- Preheat your air fryer to 320°F (160°C).

**Time:**

- Cook for 20-25 minutes until brownies are set in the center.

**Serving:**

- Makes one 9x9 inch pan of brownies.

# CONCLUSION

With these sweet treats made in your air fryer, you can satisfy your dessert cravings in no time. Whether you're enjoying crispy churros, flaky apple hand pies, homemade donuts, or gooey brownies, these recipes are sure to delight your taste buds. Get ready to impress your family and friends with these easy and tasty desserts and pastries!

# CHAPTER 27

## GUILT-FREE SNACKING: AIR-FRIED POPCORN AND CHIPS

In this chapter, we'll explore how your air fryer can be used to create guilt-free snacks like crispy popcorn and chips. Say goodbye to store-bought snacks loaded with unhealthy additives and hello to wholesome and delicious treats made right in your own kitchen. Get ready to satisfy your cravings without the guilt with these easy and tasty recipes!

## CRISPY AIR FRIED POPCORN

**Ingredients:**

- 1/4 cup popcorn kernels

- 1 tablespoon olive oil

- Salt to taste

**Machine Temperature:**

- Preheat your air fryer to 390°F (200°C).

**Time:**

- Cook for 5-7 minutes until most kernels have popped, shaking the basket occasionally.

**Serving:**

- Serves 2-3.

# FLAVORFUL AIR FRIED POTATO CHIPS

**Ingredients:**

- 2 large potatoes, thinly sliced

- 1 tablespoon olive oil

- Salt and pepper to taste

**Machine Temperature:**

- Preheat your air fryer to 360°F (180°C).

**Time:**

- Cook for 10-12 minutes until chips are golden and crispy, flipping halfway through.

**Serving:**

- Serves 2-3.

# CRISPY AIR FRIED KALE CHIPS

**Ingredients:**

- 1 bunch kale, stems removed and torn into bite-sized pieces

- 1 tablespoon olive oil

- Salt and pepper to taste

**Machine Temperature:**

- Preheat your air fryer to 350°F (175°C).

**Time:**

- Cook for 5-7 minutes until kale is crispy, shaking the basket occasionally.

**Serving:**

- Serves 2-3.

# FLAVORFUL AIR FRIED ZUCCHINI CHIPS

**Ingredients:**

- 2 medium zucchinis, thinly sliced

- 1/4 cup breadcrumbs

- 1/4 cup grated Parmesan cheese

- 1 teaspoon garlic powder

- 1/2 teaspoon paprika

- Salt and pepper to taste

**Machine Temperature:**

- Preheat your air fryer to 380°F (190°C).

**Time:**

- Cook for 8-10 minutes until chips are golden and crispy, flipping halfway through.

**Serving:**

- Serves 2-3.

# CONCLUSION

With these guilt-free snacking options made in your air fryer, you can enjoy your favorite treats without the added guilt. Whether you're munching on crispy popcorn, savory potato chips, crunchy kale chips, or flavorful zucchini chips, these recipes are sure to satisfy your cravings while keeping you on track with your healthy eating goals. Get ready to snack smarter with your air fryer!

# CHAPTER 28

## AIR-FRIED DIPS AND SPREADS

In this chapter, we'll explore how your air fryer can be used to create delicious dips and spreads that are perfect for snacking, entertaining, or adding flavor to your meals. From creamy hummus to cheesy dips, these recipes are easy to make and bursting with flavor. Get ready to elevate your dipping game with these air-fried delights!

## CRISPY AIR FRIED BUFFALO CAULIFLOWER DIP

**Ingredients:**

- 1 head cauliflower, cut into florets

- 2 tablespoons olive oil

- Salt and pepper to taste

- 1/4 cup buffalo sauce

- 1/4 cup Greek yogurt or sour cream

- 1/4 cup crumbled blue cheese

- 2 tablespoons chopped fresh parsley

**Machine Temperature:**

- Preheat your air fryer to 380°F (190°C).

**Time:**

- Cook cauliflower florets for 15-18 minutes until crispy, shaking the basket occasionally.

- In a bowl, mix buffalo sauce, Greek yogurt or sour cream, and crumbled blue cheese until well combined.

- Once cauliflower is done, toss it in the buffalo sauce mixture.

- Garnish with chopped fresh parsley and serve warm.

**Serving:**

- Serves 4-6.

# FLAVORFUL AIR FRIED GARLIC AND HERB HUMMUS

**Ingredients:**

- 1 can (15 oz) chickpeas, drained and rinsed

- 2 cloves garlic, minced

- 2 tablespoons tahini

- 2 tablespoons olive oil

- 2 tablespoons lemon juice

- 1 teaspoon dried oregano

- 1 teaspoon dried thyme

- Salt and pepper to taste

**Machine Temperature:**

- Preheat your air fryer to 350°F (175°C).

**Time:**

- Place chickpeas and minced garlic in the air fryer basket.

- Cook for 10-12 minutes until chickpeas are crispy.

- In a food processor, combine crispy chickpeas, tahini, olive oil, lemon juice, dried oregano, dried thyme, salt, and pepper.

- Blend until smooth and creamy.

- Transfer hummus to a serving bowl, drizzle with extra olive oil, and sprinkle with fresh herbs if desired.

**Serving:**

- Serves 4-6.

# CRISPY AIR FRYER SPINACH AND ARTICHOKE DIP

**Ingredients:**

- 1 cup frozen chopped spinach, thawed and drained

- 1 can (14 oz) artichoke hearts, drained and chopped

- 1 cup shredded mozzarella cheese

- 1/2 cup grated Parmesan cheese

- 1/2 cup mayonnaise

- 1/2 cup sour cream

- 1/4 cup cream cheese, softened

- 2 cloves garlic, minced

- Salt and pepper to taste

**Machine Temperature:**

- Preheat your air fryer to 370°F (185°C).

**Time:**

- In a bowl, mix together chopped spinach, chopped artichoke hearts, shredded mozzarella cheese, grated Parmesan cheese, mayonnaise, sour cream, softened cream cheese, minced garlic, salt, and pepper.

- Transfer the mixture to an oven-safe dish that fits inside your air fryer basket.

- Cook for 15-18 minutes until bubbly and golden brown.

- Serve warm with tortilla chips, crackers, or sliced baguette.

**Serving:**

- Serves 4-6.

# CONCLUSION

With these air-fried dips and spreads, you can take your snacking game to the next level. Whether you're dipping crispy cauliflower bites into buffalo dip, spreading garlic and herb hummus on pita chips, or indulging in creamy spinach and artichoke dip, these recipes are sure to impress your taste buds and your guests. Get ready to elevate your snacking experience with your air fryer!

# CHAPTER 29

## HOMEMADE SAUCES AND CONDIMENTS

In this chapter, we'll explore how your air fryer can help you create homemade sauces and condiments that are bursting with flavor and free from artificial additives. From tangy barbecue sauce to creamy aioli, these recipes will take your dishes to the next level. Get ready to elevate your meals with these easy and tasty homemade sauces and condiments!

## TANGY AIR FRIED BARBECUE SAUCE

**Ingredients:**

- 1 cup ketchup

- 1/4 cup apple cider vinegar

- 2 tablespoons brown sugar

- 1 tablespoon Worcestershire sauce

- 1 teaspoon smoked paprika

- 1/2 teaspoon garlic powder

- 1/2 teaspoon onion powder

- Salt and pepper to taste

## Machine Temperature:

- Preheat your air fryer to 350°F (175°C).

## Time:

- In a bowl, mix together all the ingredients until well combined.

- Transfer the mixture to an oven-safe dish that fits inside your air fryer basket.

- Cook for 10-12 minutes, stirring occasionally, until the sauce thickens and flavors meld together.

## Serving:

- Makes about 1 1/2 cups of barbecue sauce.

# CREAMY AIR FRIED GARLIC AIOLI

**Ingredients:**

- 1/2 cup mayonnaise

- 2 cloves garlic, minced

- 1 tablespoon lemon juice

- 1/2 teaspoon Dijon mustard

- Salt and pepper to taste

**Machine Temperature:**

- Preheat your air fryer to 350°F (175°C).

**Time:**

- In a bowl, whisk together all the ingredients until smooth and creamy.

- Transfer the mixture to an oven-safe dish that fits inside your air fryer basket.

- Cook for 8-10 minutes until the garlic is fragrant and the flavors meld together.

**Serving:**

- Makes about 1/2 cup of aioli.

# SPICY AIR FRIED SRIRACHA MAYO

**Ingredients:**

- 1/2 cup mayonnaise

- 2 tablespoons Sriracha sauce

- 1 tablespoon lime juice

- 1 teaspoon honey

- Salt and pepper to taste

**Machine Temperature:**

- Preheat your air fryer to 350°F (175°C).

**Time:**

- In a bowl, mix together all the ingredients until well combined.

- Transfer the mixture to an oven-safe dish that fits inside your air fryer basket.

- Cook for 8-10 minutes until the flavors meld together and the sauce is slightly warmed.

**Serving:**

- Makes about 1/2 cup of Sriracha mayo.

## CONCLUSION

With these homemade sauces and condiments made in your air fryer, you can enhance the flavor of any meal with ease. Whether you're slathering tangy barbecue sauce on grilled meats, dipping crispy fries into creamy aioli, or adding a kick to sandwiches with spicy Sriracha mayo, these recipes are sure to impress. Get ready to take your dishes to the next level with these easy and tasty homemade sauces and condiments!

# CHAPTER 30

## HEALTHY EATING WITH AIR FRYER

In this chapter, we'll explore how the air fryer can be your ally in maintaining a healthy diet without sacrificing flavor. From lighter versions of classic favorites to creative and nutritious meals, these recipes will help you make healthier choices while still enjoying delicious food. Get ready to embark on a journey of healthy eating with your air fryer!

# CRISPY AIR FRIED VEGGIE CHIPS

**Ingredients:**

- 1 large sweet potato, thinly sliced

- 1 large beet, thinly sliced

- 1 large carrot, thinly sliced

- 1 tablespoon olive oil

- Salt and pepper to taste

**Machine Temperature:**

- Preheat your air fryer to 375°F (190°C).

**Time:**

- Cook for 10-12 minutes until chips are golden and crispy, flipping halfway through.

**Serving:**

- Serves 2-3.

# FLAVORFUL AIR FRYER LEMON HERB SALMON

**Ingredients:**

- 2 salmon fillets

- 2 tablespoons olive oil

- 2 cloves garlic, minced

- Zest and juice of 1 lemon

- 1 tablespoon chopped fresh parsley

- 1 tablespoon chopped fresh dill

- Salt and pepper to taste

- Lemon wedges for serving

## Machine Temperature:

- Preheat your air fryer to 380°F (190°C).

## Time:

- Rub salmon fillets with olive oil, minced garlic, lemon zest, lemon juice, chopped parsley, chopped dill, salt, and pepper.

- Place salmon fillets in the air fryer basket.

- Cook for 8-10 minutes until salmon is cooked through and flakes easily with a fork.

## Serving:

- Serves 2.

# CRISPY AIR FRIED CHICKEN BREAST WITH MIXED GREENS

**Ingredients:**

- 2 boneless, skinless chicken breasts

- 2 tablespoons olive oil

- 1 teaspoon garlic powder

- 1 teaspoon paprika

- Salt and pepper to taste

- 4 cups mixed greens

- 1 tablespoon balsamic vinegar

- 1 tablespoon olive oil

**Machine Temperature:**

- Preheat your air fryer to 380°F (190°C).

**Time:**

- Rub chicken breasts with olive oil, garlic powder, paprika, salt, and pepper.

- Place chicken breasts in the air fryer basket.

- Cook for 15-18 minutes until chicken is cooked through and juices run clear.

- In a bowl, toss mixed greens with balsamic vinegar and olive oil.

- Serve crispy chicken breasts with mixed greens on the side.

**Serving:**

- Serves 2.

# CONCLUSION

With these healthy recipes made in your air fryer, you can enjoy nutritious and flavorful meals without the guilt. Whether you're munching on crispy veggie chips, savoring lemon herb salmon, or enjoying crispy chicken breast with mixed greens, these recipes are sure to satisfy your cravings while keeping you on track with your healthy eating goals. Get ready to make healthier choices with your air fryer and embark on a journey of delicious and nutritious meals!

Made in the USA
Monee, IL
18 November 2024

70441112R00092